LIGHTNING BOLT BOOKS™

Blue Everywhere

Kristin Sterling

Lerner Publications Company
Minneapolis

Is your favorite color blue? This book is dedicated to YOU.

Lerner Publications Company
A division of Lerner Publishing Group, Inc.
241 First Avenue North
Minneapolis, MN 55401 U.S.A.

Website address: www.lernerbooks.com

Library of Congress Cataloging-in-Publication Data

Sterling, Kristin.
    Blue Everywhere / by Kristin Sterling.
        p.   cm. — (Lightning bolt books™—Colors everywhere)
    Includes bibliographical references and index.
    ISBN 978-0-7613-4588-6 (lib. bdg. : alk. paper)
    1. Blue—Juvenile literature. 2. Colors—Juvenile literature. I. Title.
    QC495.5.S745 2010
    535.6—dc22   2009017985

Manufactured in the United States of America
1 — BP — 12/15/09

Contents

A Relaxing World

Do you like cool, calm colors? Many people love the color blue.

Blue things can be found in nature. Let's see if we can find a few!

This flower and butterfly are shades of blue.

The sky is a bright, bold
blue on sunny summer days.
Clouds float across the sky
like fluffy pillows.

The water is blue in the wide, open ocean. Dolphins splash and play in the waves.

Bottlenose dolphins leap from blue ocean waters.

Forget-me-nots
are blue flowers.
They bloom in
the shade.

8

Some parrots are a brilliant blue color.

This bird lives in South America.

The hyacinth macaw is a kind of parrot.

People pick
blueberries
when they
are ripe on
the bush.
What a
tasty treat!

Sapphires
are pretty blue
gemstones. They
can be worn
as jewelry.

This necklace has
blue sapphires and
white diamonds.

Blue things are also made by people. Jeans are blue denim pants.

Jeans are comfortable, sturdy clothes for relaxing or playing outside.

People wear blue makeup.

Cars are painted blue.

Blue Hues

Blue comes in many shades, or hues. Can you think of some?

Baby blue is a light shade of blue. Patrick is under a baby blue blanket.

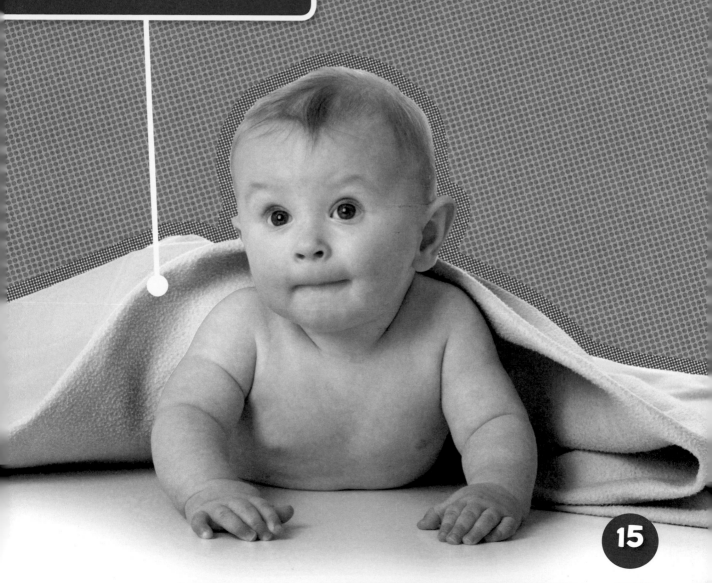

The light shade of this blanket is also called pastel blue.

Navy blue is a dark shade of blue. Jenny's dress is navy blue.

Turquoise is
the name of
a blue green
color. Doli
is wearing
a turquoise
necklace.

Jewelry made with turquoise stones is popular in some American Indian cultures.

Periwinkle is a beautiful purplish shade of blue. This flower is periwinkle.

Periwinkle is the name of this flower and this color.

Feeling Blue?

Sometimes people say that they are feeling blue. What does this mean?

Are they cold?
Is their skin turning blue?

This girl's face and lips are painted with a blue design.

B.B. King is a famous blues musician.

No! When people say they're feeling blue, it means they're sad. When people sing the blues, they sing about what makes them sad.

Do you think
blue is a sad
color?

Becky Loves Blue

Becky does not think blue is a sad color. She loves it!

Becky wears blue clothes from head to foot. She even has blue eyes.

Blue is her favorite color. She loves to eat blue cotton candy.

Cotton candy is often blue or pink.

Her bedroom is blue, and it makes her feel happy.

Would you like a blue bedroom?

What is your favorite color?

Activity
You Can Blend Colors

Blue is a primary color. This means that you cannot blend other colors together to make blue. Red and yellow are also primary colors. You can blend blue, yellow, and red to make other colors.

What you need:
three paintbrushes
blue paint
yellow paint
red paint
a paper plate or
    palette
a cup of water
white construction
    paper or a canvas

What you do:

1. Use the paintbrushes to mix together blue and yellow paint on a plate or palette. Blue and yellow make green.

2. Wash your paintbrushes in a cup of water.

3. Blend yellow and red paint on another part of the plate or palette. Red and yellow make orange.

4. Wash your paintbrushes in a cup of water.

5. Mix together blue and red paint on a clean part of the plate or palette. Blue and red make purple.

6. Create a painting on a sheet of construction paper or canvas using the primary colors and the colors you have made.

7. Put your painting on the refrigerator so everyone can see it!

Glossary

bloom: when a plant's flowers open

blues: sad songs about a person's problems

brilliant: very bright

calm: peaceful

hue: the darkness of a color

nature: everything in the world that is not made by people

palette: a thin board on which artists can mix paints

primary color: a color that cannot be made by mixing other colors

Further Reading

Color Crafts for Kids
http://www.cool-kids-craft-ideas.com/color-crafts.html

Learn about Color!
http://www.metmuseum.org/explore/Learn_About_Color/index.html

Onyefulu, Ifeoma. *Chidi Only Likes Blue: An African Book of Colours.* London: Frances Lincoln Children's Books, 2006.

Ross, Kathy. *Kathy Ross Crafts Colors.* Minneapolis: Millbrook Press, 2003.

Tashiro, Chisato. *Chameleon's Colors.* New York: North-South Books, 2007.

Wood, Audrey. *The Deep Blue Sea: A Book of Colors.* New York: Blue Sky Press, 2005.

Index

Photo Acknowledgments

The images in this book are used with the permission of: © Marek Kosmal/Dreamstime. com, p. 1; © Brad Wilson/Stone/Getty Images, p. 2; © Jim Esposito/The Image Bank/ Getty Images, p. 4; © Dragoneye/Dreamstime.com, p. 5; © Tim Flach/Stone/Getty Images, p. 6; © Duncan Noakes/Dreamstime.com, p. 7; © Peter Lilja/Taxi/Getty Images, p. 8; © Bonnie Pignatiello Leer/Dreamstime.com, p. 9; © Andersen Ross/Blend Images/ Getty Images, p. 10; © SuperStock/SuperStock, p. 11; © Nick Daly/Digital Vision/Getty Images, p. 12; © Clarissa Leahy/Taxi/Getty Images, p. 13; © Ron Levine/The Image Bank/Getty Images, p. 14; © iStockphoto.com/Jaroslaw Wojcik, p. 15; © Shinya Sasaki/ NEOVISION/Getty Images, p. 16; © Scott T. Baxter/Photodisc/Getty Images, p. 17; © iStockphoto.com/Sergey Chushkin , p. 18; © Westend61/SuperStock, p. 19; © Kre_geg/ Dreamstime.com, p. 20; © Bob Levey/WireImage/Getty Images, p. 21; © Superstudio/ The Image Bank/Getty Images, p. 22; © Rayes/Digital Vision/Getty Images, pp. 23, 24; © Lora Clark –Fotolia.com, p. 25; © Wildscape/Alamy, p. 26; © Jack Hollingsworth/ Dreamstime.com, p. 27; © Hill Creek Pictures/SuperStock, p. 28; © Diman Oshchepkov/ Dreamstime.com, p. 30; © Jose Luis Pelaez/Iconica/Getty Images, p. 31.

Front cover: © Alexmax/Dreamstime.com (jeans); © Diman Oshchepkov/Dreamstime. com (fish); © Pkruger/Dreamstime.com (blueberries); © Oldclimber/Dreamstime.com (bird); © iStockphoto.com/Sergey Chushkin (flower); © Todd Strand/Independent Picture Service (paint strips).